My First Book of

Colors

AND

Shapes

Learning Fun for Toddlers

ROCKRIDGE
PRESS

First Rockridge Press hardcover edition 2022

Originally published in trade paperback by Rockridge Press 2021

Rockridge Press and the Rockridge Press logo are trademarks or registered trademarks of Callisto Media Inc. and/or its affiliates in the United States and other countries and may not be used without written permission.

For general information on our other products and services, please contact our Customer Care Department within the United States at (866) 744-2665, or outside the United States at (510) 253-0500.

Hardcover ISBN: 979-8-88608-391-0
Paperback ISBN: 978-1-64876-582-7
eBook ISBN: 978-1-64876-726-5

Manufactured in the United States of America

Interior and Cover Designer: John Calmeyer
Art Producer: Sara Feinstein
Editor: Laura Bryn Sisson
Production Editor: Mia Moran
Production Manager: Jose Olivera

Photography used under license from Shutterstock.com

10 9 8 7 6 5 4 3 2 1 0

Dear Reader,

Learning shapes and colors is such an exciting step in your child's development!

This book is designed to grow with your child. Your child will progress from learning basic shapes and colors to identifying these shapes and colors in their environment.

To help your child learn, try these tips:

- Point to and name the pictures your child is looking at or touching. You can say, "Yes, a circle. A yellow circle. Just like the sun!"

- Ask your child questions about what they notice on the page. You can ask, "What do you see?" or "What else is a square?"

- Use everyday objects of different colors and shapes to reinforce your child's learning. Start by showing your toddler how the shapes and colors match what's on the page, then ask your child to try.

Use this book to read, learn, play, and enjoy quality time with your child over and over again.

**red
circle**

**red
square**

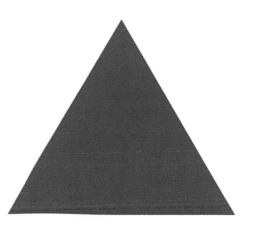

red rectangle

red triangle

red apple

red fire truck

**orange
circle**

**orange
square**

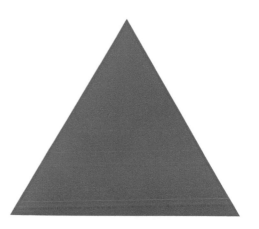

**orange
rectangle**

**orange
triangle**

orange carrot

orange pumpkin

yellow
circle

yellow
square

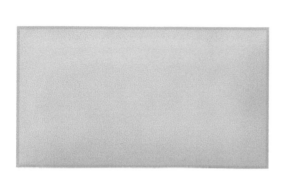

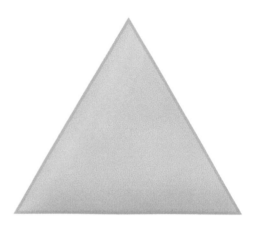

**yellow
rectangle**

**yellow
triangle**

yellow banana

yellow chick

green circle

green square

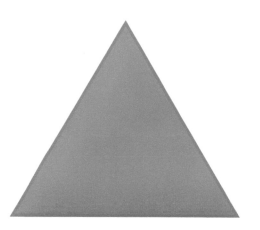

**green
rectangle**

**green
triangle**

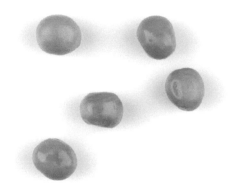

green peas

green frog

**blue
circle**

**blue
square**

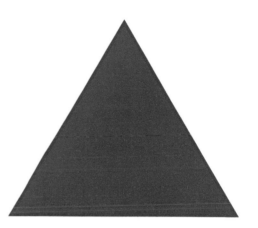

**blue
rectangle**

**blue
triangle**

blue blueberries

blue ball

**purple
circle**

**purple
square**

purple rectangle

purple triangle

purple grapes

purple socks

**pink
circle**

**pink
square**

**pink
rectangle**

**pink
triangle**

pink crayon

pink pig

white circle

white square

white rectangle

white triangle

white dog

white cloud

black circle

black square

**black
rectangle**

**black
triangle**

black cat

black train

**brown
circle**

**brown
square**

**brown
rectangle**

**brown
triangle**

brown cow

brown cookie

red circle

blue square

brown rectangle

green triangle

pink heart

purple star

white oval

orange cone

yellow diamond

brown crescent

BOW!

More books for your toddler library

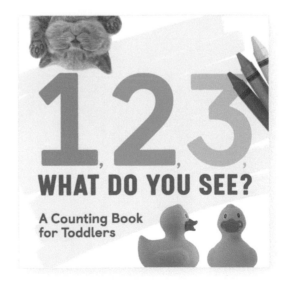